T0083208

Wend Your Way

A BUR OAK GUIDE

# Wend Your Way

A Guide to Sites along the Iowa Mormon Trail

L. Matthew Chatterley

*with a foreword by Susan Easton Black*

University of Iowa Press, Iowa City

University of Iowa Press, Iowa City 52242

www.uiowapress.org

Copyright © 2000 by Iowa State University Press

Printed in the United States of America

First University of Iowa Press edition, 2010

No part of this book may be reproduced or used in any
form or by any means without permission in writing from
the publisher. All reasonable steps have been taken to contact
copyright holders of material used in this book. The publisher
would be pleased to make suitable arrangements with any
whom it has not been possible to reach.

The University of Iowa Press is a member of Green Press Initiative
and is committed to preserving natural resources.

Printed on acid-free paper

Library of Congress Cataloging-in-Publication Data

Chatterley, L. Matthew.

Wend your way: a guide to sites along the Iowa Mormon Trail /
L. Matthew Chatterley; with a foreword by Susan Easton Black.—
1st University of Iowa Press ed.

p.   cm.—(A Bur Oak guide)

Originally published: Ames, Iowa: Iowa State University Press,
2000.

Includes bibliographical references.

ISBN-13: 978-1-58729-571-3 (pbk.)

ISBN-10: 1-58729-571-7 (pbk.)

1. Mormon pioneers—Iowa—History—19th century.

2. Mormons—Iowa—History—19th century.   3. Frontier and
pioneer life—Iowa.   4. Iowa—History—19th century.

5. Mormon Pioneer National Historic Trail—Guidebooks.

6. Iowa—Guidebooks.   7. Historic sites—Iowa—Guidebooks.
I. Title.

F630.M8 C48  2007        2007020506

977.7'020882893—dc22

# Contents

# Acknowledgments

*Wend Your Way: A Guide to Sites Along the Iowa Mormon Trail* tells the general story of the Mormons' movement across Iowa on their way to a home in the Great Basin of the West. This work includes a discussion of and directions to wayside exhibits along the Mormon Trail in Iowa constructed in 1996 by the U.S. National Park Service and the Iowa Mormon Trails Association.

Those who are interested in this part of Iowa's history can visit more than 30 marked locations significant to the monumental exodus. Hopefully, *Wend Your Way: A Guide to Sites Along the Iowa Mormon Trail* will help lead them to these locations, many of which previously have been difficult to find.

A general historical discussion is included, which is meant primarily as a reminder or introduction to the events that happened in 1846. This book also reproduces in one place the illustrations found on the National Park Service exhibits and includes maps and directions to trail markers and other sites of interest across Iowa.

This work would not have been completed without the encouragement of many friends and colleagues. Nor would it have been possible without the previous labor, interest and support of many Iowans and others committed to finding and celebrating remnants of the Iowa portion of the Mormon Trail.

First, I am most indebted to my family. My wife, Ruth, and our children, Arianne and her husband (Lance Morgan), Amanda, Brad, Greg, Maja and Kathryn, have supported and encouraged my efforts in this work. Ruth has been my companion as we have traveled the trail our ancestors traversed generations before us. She has willingly accepted additional responsibilities so that I might complete this project.

Second, I am grateful to my associates of the Iowa Mormon Trails Association (IMTA) for their encouragement and support. The IMTA and the U.S. National Park Service initially asked me to create drawings for interpretive panels being prepared as part of the trail's sesquicentennial celebration. The panels were designed for sites in each of the southern Iowa counties traversed by the trail. My body of work was a task of love that took nearly a year to complete and brought me closer than any previous study or contemplation to those who participated in this greatest of western migrations.

As an artist, to be able to visualize and depict scenes and participants symbolic of events pivotal to my own faith and heritage was a privilege and opportunity I did not take lightly. I am thankful to the people who were part of that portion of this project: William and Sid Price, public affairs missionaries for the Church of Jesus Christ of Latter-day Saints who helped coordinate events associated with the sesquicentennial celebration; Kay Threlkeld, of the National Park Service's Long Distance Trails Office; William G. Hartley, historian who offered suggestions for historical detail; and Delores Berklund, president of the IMTA.

The IMTA later commissioned me to create maps for a brochure on the wayside exhibits in Iowa. Those maps were the genesis of the ones found in this work. This book is an expansion of the earlier brochure in several ways. Some of the drawings found on the interpretive panels were reproduced in the brochure, but in this work all are printed in one location for the first time. The book follows a format similar to the brochure, breaking up the text into information for each county. It also includes information about other sites in southern Iowa that might be of interest or useful to the traveler.

I am constantly in awe of the members of the Iowa Mormon Trails Association. They are committed to the trail because it has touched their lives and their land—the land they love and call home. Though they are not descendants of the early travelers, they have spent time and resources to preserve the legacy the emigrants left across Iowa. Their work has made this work possible and will allow thousands to be touched by the sacrifices those early pioneers made in the state. My appreciation is expressed to Delores and Bill Berklund, Jane Briley, Paul and Karla Gunzenhouser, Bob Brown, Don Smith, Don Reasoner, Valda Kennedy, Jean Wampler, Leon Wilkinson, D. Elbert Pidcock and many others associated with the Iowa Mormon Trails Association.

Third, I am grateful for the encouragement and suggestions of Susan Easton Black and for the contribution of her foreword to this book. Her tireless devotion and monumental efforts dedicated to the pioneers who traveled, built, suffered and sometimes died along the Mormon Trail are an inspiration and unparalleled in historic scholarship.

Fourth, I express my appreciation to other family members, friends and associates who have been supportive of me and my love for Iowa and the trail: Dennis and Nancy Lowman, Karen and Steven Herwig, William and Nila Siddoway, Loren and Annette Burton, Darlene Hutchison, Joe Cheney, Stanley and Stella Welsh, Louis and Sandra Chatterley, Chuck Offenberger and Randy Evans.

I gratefully acknowledge the interest of Iowa State University Press in pursuing publication of this book. It is fitting that it should publish this work. The events described took place on Iowa soil and are a rich part of the history of this land. Current interest in the trail was kindled and is fed by Iowans living adjacent to it. My family is forever tied to Iowa. Though my childhood roots are in the West, I am rooted in Iowa soil by ancestors who crossed the state in 1846; by my professional career as an artist and journalist at the *Des Moines Register*; by my father-in-law, who brought his family to Ames years ago while earning a doctorate in botany from Iowa State University; and by my children, who are privileged to have been raised and educated in this great state.

Finally, I am grateful to the pioneers, my ancestors among them, who suffered and struggled across the plains and hills of southern Iowa on their way to the Missouri River and the Great Basin of the West. Their example is an inspiration to all who learn of their toil and sacrifice. Today you can walk along portions of the trail still accessible in Iowa and feel the strength of the words of William Clayton written in the spring of 1846 at a camp south of present-day Corydon. The message is still hopeful and comforting:

Come, come ye Saints
No toil nor labor fear
But with joy, wend your way
Though hard to you this journey may appear
Grace shall be as your day.

'Tis better far for us to strive
Our useless cares from us to drive
Do this and joy, your hearts will swell
All is well! All is well!

Why should we mourn or think our lot is hard?
'Tis not so, all is right
Why should we think to earn a great reward
If we now shun the fight?

Gird up your loins, fresh courage take
Our God will never us forsake
Do this and joy, your hearts will swell
All is well! All is well!

We'll find the place which God for us prepared
Far away in the West
Where none shall come to hurt or make afraid
There the Saints will be blessed.

We'll make the air with music ring
Shout praises to our God and King
Above the rest these words we'll tell
All is well! All is well!

And should we die before our journey's through
Happy day! All is well!
We then are free from toil and sorrow too
With the just we shall dwell.

But if our lives are spared again
To see the Saints their rest obtain
Oh how we'll make this chorus swell
All is well! All is well!

# FOREWORD

*Susan Easton Black, distinguished professor,*
*Department of Church History and Doctrine, Brigham Young University*

In the history of Iowa, 1846 remains the seminal year. In that year statehood was declared and the Iowa Mormon Trail was carved across the southern tier of the state. Of these two events, studies of the historic trail pale in comparison to the process of achieving statehood for most readers, but to the descendants of Mormon pioneers who traversed the glacial hills of Iowa on their epic trek to the West and to historians who study the suffering of this religious community, the story of the Iowa Mormon Trail is unparalleled.

The saga of the Iowa Mormon Trail began on the fourth of February, 1846, when Charles Shumway crossed the Mississippi River from Nauvoo, Illinois, and entered Lee County. His river skiff landing was soon followed by thousands of other Mormon landings, bringing families of persecuted coreligionists seeking refuge from the hatred and intolerance they had known in Illinois. Many of them were unprepared, poorly clad and lacked provisions and wagons. But it seems that most of the Mormon exiles were convinced that the faith they embraced was worth any inconvenience or sacrifice. Their courage stemmed from a conviction that the Lord was guiding their westward movement.

"I am glad the time of our exodus has come; I have looked for it for years," penned Mormon leader Heber C. Kimball. "There may be individuals who will look at their pretty houses and gardens [in Illinois] and say, 'it is hard to leave them,' but I tell you, when we start, you will put on your knapsacks and follow after us."[1]

And follow they did. The sudden emergence of multitudes of Mormons camping in southern Iowa caused many Iowans to worry and even fear the "Mormon invasion." Few were concerned that the Mormons were finding the crossing of Iowa a most difficult segment in their migration. Instead their concern was for the welfare of their own families as unsupported rumors brought waves of fear for life and home. According to the *Bloomington Herald,* "Public meeting[s] were held so that Iowans could take measure to protect themselves from the Mormons."[2] But such protection proved unwarranted. The Mormons were not a menace to society, warlike or even rowdy. They were merely refugees seeking relief from the trials that had beset them in Illinois. They were not frontiersmen hoping for adventure or adventurers seeking gold, verdant fields or prosperity. They weren't even hoping to spread the realm of the United States from sea to sea in fulfillment of the politically popular doctrine of manifest destiny.

The Mormons were families seeking solace and momentary respite on the soil of Iowa. They traveled in clusters, sharing their meager supplies, expenses and equipment. Their experience in southern Iowa appears similar to that of other pioneering families crossing the state. Written accounts of muddy ground, frozen clothes and deep rivers are plentiful in their diaries. Fear of Indians, wild animals and sickness dominate much of their writings as do dramatic recitations of struggling for shelter and food. But the most consistent entry is of livestock, wagons and walking—and walking again.

The one significant difference between the Mormon journal accounts and those written by other pioneering factions was the Mormon belief that God was guiding them. This belief was so strong that "the possibility of being left behind was more distressing than the weather, the short provisions, or difficulty in travel."[3] And so with belief as the motivation, they kept coming.

One by one they crossed the Mississippi River and with wagon and oxen trekked through southern Iowa. Their growing numbers and their intense suffering has captured the fancy of proud descendants and historians of the western movement. Their example in Iowa of fortitude, perseverance and endurance is still told around campfires, in family gatherings and in classrooms throughout the state. The retelling of their herculean courage amid great obstacles has led many a child and even an adult to claim the Mormon pioneers in Iowa as heroes and heroines.

Such acclamation about a persecuted people has led more than one historian to remember the Mormon experience in Iowa by mapping, marking and preserving the Mormon Trail. Yet by 1900, most earlier memorial efforts were nearly obliterated by farms that mushroomed over the route. Edgar Harlan, state archivist, was one of a growing number of historians who wanted to identify the ghost remnants of the vanishing trail. He spent many hours locating and marking the trail and then strongly advised the Daughters of the American Revolution to erect stone and bronze monuments at key sites along the route.

Following the lead of Harlan, the Civil Conservation Corps in the 1930s added an additional hundred wooden Mormon Trail signs to mark the trail. Forty years later in the 1970s, the trail was again marked. The Mormon Pioneer Trail Foundation and the state of Iowa placed blue and white signs along highways in southern Iowa. It was during this marking that the president of the United States, Jimmy Carter, officially named the trail the Mormon Pioneer National Historic Trail. In his naming of the trail, President Carter asked that the Department of Interior and the National Park Service preserve the trail for generations to enjoy and remember.

In keeping with the presidential charge, the National Park Service placed brown and white triangular signs that read "Mormon Pioneer National Historic Trail" along the state highway. Then in 1996, in commemoration of the 150th anniversaries of the Iowa Mormon Trail and Iowa statehood, the National Park Service, the state of Iowa, and the Iowa Mormon Trails Association placed more than two dozen wayside panel exhibits on the historic trail.

As members of these important agencies searched for an artist to depict the Mormon experience on each exhibit, it is not surprising that the name Matthew Chatterley, a senior artist of *The Des Moines Register*, emerged as first choice. Chatterley had established a fine reputation in illustration, mapmaking and graphic presentation that has been enjoyed by readers of *The Des Moines Register* for years. He was not only skilled as a graphic artist but had an unusual appreciation for the historical importance of place. He knew that the Mormon Pioneer National Historic Trail through Iowa was worth marking and attempting to preserve one more time.

His artistic talent and his lifelong pursuit to remember the Mormon experience brought him to the attention of Iowa state and local leaders. Although a modest man as to his own importance, what he achieved in southern Iowa is not of modest proportions. He helped preserve Iowa's trail history by creating intimate visual depictions for markers that now dot the landscape of 12 Iowa counties. For his contribution, his name will be spoken along with that of Edgar Harlan. But there is a difference between the men—Chatterley hoped for a permanent remembrance of the Iowa trail.

Knowing from past experience that markers are too often destroyed by weather, graffiti, bullet holes and time, he determined to create a permanent remembrance of the Mormon pioneers crossing Iowa. The form of choice for Chatterley was to write a book that highlighted the brief narrative and artistic renderings depicted on the interpretive panels alongside the trail. The reader of *Wend Your Way* will quickly be convinced that Chatterley accomplished his task.

Readers will find in *Wend Your Way* trail maps, photographs, depictions of markers and informative descriptions of Mormon sites reflective of the interpretive roadside panels. Although Chatterley is true to the highest standards of scholarship and objectivity in his reporting of the trail counties, his love for the trail and the Mormon pioneers is apparent on every page. His sectional groupings are organized geographically and sequenced from east to west so the reader can vicariously move directionally alongside the Mormon pioneers.

*Wend Your Way* begins with highlights of the Mormons in Nauvoo, Illinois. Emphasis is appropriately placed on the famed Nauvoo Temple and the martyrdom of Mormon leader Joseph Smith. The author then details for the reader the difficulty of moving a religiously persecuted people from their Nauvoo homes to political safety across the Mississippi River and into adjacent Lee County. After finishing his Lee

County narrative, Chatterley writes of a commemorative wayside exhibit at the ferryboat landing and of another at the Linger Longer Park, north of Montrose. Clear directions to these exhibits can guide interested Iowans and travelers. But for the reader, it will be the art that will arrest a quick turn of the page. The sketches are simple, yet poignant. They appear as if the reader were privileged to view drawings done by a Mormon pioneer sitting on the tongue of a wagon.

Chatterley then follows the Mormons into Van Buren County and briefly discusses the hardships faced by the exiles as they struggled to find shelter and food in bitter, wintry conditions. Again the author makes note of the important local sites and includes a representative picture, map and directions to the interpretive panel. But once again, it is the artist renderings that will capture the reader's attention.

The reader will soon discover that the brief word sketches in *Wend Your Way* are as reflective of the Mormon pioneers as are the drawings. Chatterley's chapter subtitles are often taken from the sites' interpretive panels, such as "Magic City of the Woods," which describes the Garden Grove settlement. The reader will be enticed by these subtitles and connected to the trail markers.

As Chatterley moves through the state from county to county, his consistent presentation of material will be assuring to the reader that the author is more than just superficially conversant about the trail. The blend of explanations of the Mormon experience in each county, directions to the interpretive panels, maps and other sites significant to the Mormon pioneer experience make for easy reading. But for those traversing the trail, it will make locating such significant sites as the Chariton River camp and the Shoal Creek camp not only probable, but possible.

Although Chatterley will be primarily remembered for his artistic renderings and descriptive writing of *Wend Your Way*, his photographs should not be ignored. The photographs document the 1996 reenactment of the exodus along the Iowa Mormon Trail and give new life to pioneering events that occurred more than 150 years ago.

I express gratitude to Matthew Chatterley for his fond remembrance of the thousands of Mormon pioneers who left their homes in

Illinois to enter Iowa. Although other guidebooks of southern Iowa are useful and each makes a contribution, Chatterley has captured information from the interpretive panels and sketches that convey a new historical perspective for southern Iowa. I express gratitude to the author for preserving the Mormon heritage in the Hawkeye state.

## NOTES

1. *Times and Seasons*, Nauvoo, Illinois, November 6, 1845.
2. *Bloomington Herald*, Bloomington, Illinois, July 5, 1845; see also October 25 and November 15, 1845.
3. Carol Cornwall Madsen, "'But with Joy Wend Your Way': Women on the Iowa Mormon Trail," *The Iowa Mormon Trail: Legacy of Faith and Courage*, ed. Susan Easton Black and William G. Hartley (Orem, Utah: Helix Publishing, 1997), p. 114.

# WEND YOUR WAY

# INTRODUCTION
## *Leaving Nauvoo the Beautiful*

In 1839 the Mormons began moving into the area of Commerce, Illinois, on the eastern bank of the Mississippi River. Forced to leave settlements in Missouri, they drained the swampy bottomlands adjacent to the river and began to build a new American city.

Their industrious building program was evidence of long-range visions, hopes and dreams for this place. Large squares of real estate were divided in orderly fashion. Industries were established to aid growth and development. Beautiful brick homes were built. A local limestone quarry provided stone for construction of a magnificent structure on the hill overlooking the bend in the river. The structure, a

Replica of the Nauvoo Temple

Latter-day temple, became the crowning gem of the new community and the focus of its work and industry.

The city was named Nauvoo, a Hebrew word meaning "beautiful place." It was the gathering place for converts who embraced a new American religion, and they poured in by the thousands. At its center was the charismatic Joseph Smith—mayor of Nauvoo, general of the city's militia, president of the church, translator of an ancient religious record and prophet to a people.

But the Mormons' hope for a peaceful existence in western Illinois was short-lived. Its growth from a few scattered cabins to one of the largest cities in the United States with a population of about 12,000 created fear and distrust in some. Misunderstandings, growth of political and economic power, and the inflammatory claims of enemies of the young church fed a mob mentality that led to the murder of Joseph Smith and his brother Hyrum in Carthage, Illinois, on June 27, 1844.

Joseph Smith's enemies hoped his death would also kill Mormonism. Instead, the Mormons renamed Nauvoo "The City of Joseph" in his honor and sustained Brigham Young as their new leader. Brigham's continued missionary zeal and dedication to completing the temple Joseph had begun inspired and solidified the people. So the fear and distrust of neighbors, some with political power in the state of Illinois, continued.

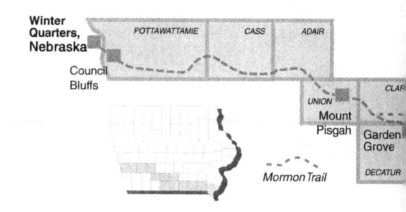

Squares indicate prominent camp sites

Carthage Jail, Carthage, Illinois

Eventually, the inhabitants of "The City of Joseph" realized their only safety lay in deserting their beloved city and seeking freedom from persecution in the mountains of the West. They planned to leave in the spring of 1846. However, political pressure caused them to move sooner than originally planned. On a frigid day in early February, the first wagons made their way across the Mississippi River and began their journey across Iowa and toward a new home in the West.

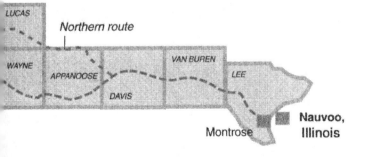

# LEE COUNTY
*Where the Exodus Began*

For many, Lee County, Iowa, was the first faithful step in the Mormons' monumental migration from Nauvoo to the Great Basin in the West. It is appropriately known as where the exodus began.

The 1846 migration took place in three waves. The first occurred in winter and included some 3,000 people who accompanied Brigham Young. Their route across Iowa is remembered as the "official" Mormon Trail. The second wave occurred in spring and was, by far, the largest part of the exodus. Approximately 10,000 Saints from Nauvoo and adjacent communities, including several on the Iowa side of the Mississippi River, participated in this part of the migration. (At its peak, Nauvoo had a population of around 12,000 people. Another 3,000 Mormons lived in nearby Illinois and Iowa settlements.) The third wave left Nauvoo in the fall of 1846. This group consisted of nearly 1,000 of the poorest of the Saints—those who did not have means to leave with the other groups—and those who had been too ill to travel. Forced from Nauvoo by vigilantes, their retreat left Nauvoo essentially abandoned.

A wayside exhibit at the ferryboat landing site in Montrose recognizes the starting point of the Iowa trail and the Saints' first steps on

Looking toward Montrose, Lee County, Iowa, from Parley Street, Nauvoo, Illinois

Iowa soil. Most of the wagons, teams and supplies were ferried across the river to this point. Wagons were able to cross the river on the ice for a short period of time following a freeze on February 24. The illustration on the exhibit that appears at the beginning of this chapter shows a mother and son assisting in the crossing.

At this point in 1846 the Mississippi River was much shallower and narrower than it is today. Locks and dams now exist above and below Nauvoo, adding to the depth and breadth of the river for the benefit of barge traffic.

Once the Mississippi was crossed, the Saints gathered in the timber and bottoms of Sugar Creek about eight miles west of the river.

A second wayside exhibit exists at Linger Longer Park, a little north of Montrose. This interpretive panel shown at the end of this chapter celebrates the experience of the last group of 1846 emigrants, the "camp of the poor," after they were forced from Nauvoo in the fall, several months after the exodus began. The indigent camp of 500 to 600 people was destitute. Many were sick or on the brink of starvation. Thomas Bullock wrote in his diary on October 9, "A large, or rather several large, flocks of quails flew into camp. Some fell on the wagons, some under, some on the breakfast tables. The boys and brethren ran about after them and caught them alive with their hands. Men who were not in the church marvelled at the sight. ... The boys caught about 20 alive and as to the number that were killed, every man, woman and child had quails to eat for their dinner."

### Pioneer Camps in Lee County

*Sugar Creek camp 1* (February 4–28). The Saints camped here during the month of February, and leaders went back and forth making preparations for the exodus. The site is near the town of Argyle. From Highway 218, go west 5.3 miles on county road J72 to where Sugar Creek crosses the road.

*Sugar Creek camp 2* (March 1). Northwest of camp 1, a few miles on the west side of Sugar Creek.

*Lick Creek camp* (March 2). This site is near the town of Croton and east of the Des Moines River.

### Other Sites of Interest in Lee County

*Old Fort Madison.* A historic fort located at Riverview Park in Fort Madison.

*Rand Park, Keokuk.* This park has picnic and playground facilities with a magnificent view of the Mississippi River. It is at 17th Street and Grand Avenue in Keokuk.

*Shimek State Forest.* This is a beautiful state forest abounding in heavy oak timber adjacent to Highway 2 on the western edge of the county.

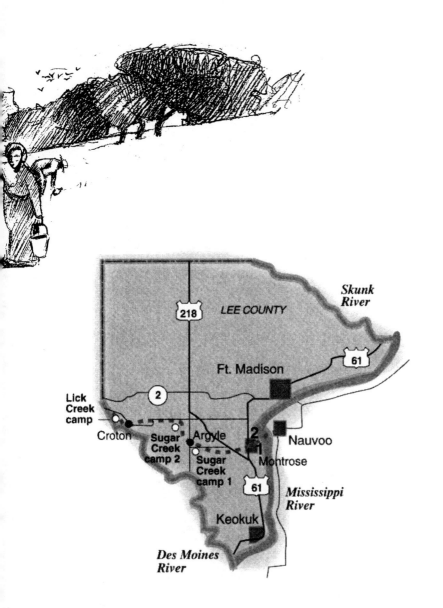

## DIRECTIONS TO INTERPRETIVE PANELS IN LEE COUNTY

1. In Montrose, leave U.S. Highway 61 and turn east on Highway 404, go one mile and cross the railroad tracks to Riverview Park on the Mississippi River.

2. From Riverview Park, exit across the railroad tracks to the stop sign and turn right. Linger Longer Park is just south of Highway 61.

# Van Buren County

*From Ice to Mud*

The first wave of Saints, which included many of the church leadership, began their journey across Iowa in the extreme conditions of Iowa's winter. Bitter cold snow and—as winter changed to early spring—ice accompanied their trek. Ice storms occur occasionally during early spring in Iowa. When the ground is at freezing, or below, but the temperature of the air above is warmer, precipitation begins as rain. But as soon as the rain contacts the ground, it freezes and coats everything it touches with a layer of ice. Imagine the pioneers waking in the morning to find ice coating everything in camp! Imagine trying to start a fire, prepare breakfast or take care of a sick child in such conditions. Imagine laying down to sleep at night and in the morning being unable to rise because your clothes are frozen to the ground.

As spring continued, icy conditions changed to mud. Spring rains were often and heavy. Mud became a constant opponent of the Saints' progress. It mired animals, broke wagon axles and caused travelers to lighten their loads by abandoning unnecessary belongings. Spring rains filled riverbanks with raging brown currents that made crossings dangerous or impossible. And bringing wagons up steep banks after the river crossing was slippery and tricky. One journal entry stated it took 25 yoke of oxen hooked to one wagon to get it up out of the river.

The wayside exhibit near the old flour mill in Bonaparte and the illustration at the beginning of this chapter show the struggle of the

Crossing of the Des Moines River at Bonaparte

Saints with muddy roads, including the circumstance for women. The mud and moisture crept up from their hems until their skirts were soaked and walking was nearly impossible. The panel, in Riverfront Park, is directly across from the site where the pioneers crossed the Des Moines River.

The pioneers traveled across roads already established through most of Van Buren County, which was already settled in several areas. They capitalized on the situation and spread throughout the area offering work for money and supplies to help them on their journey. Many of the early cabins and buildings in the county were built by Mormon craftsmen; some of them are still standing. According to Ralph Arnold, Van Buren County historian, the Mason House Inn in Bentonsport was most likely built by Mormons in 1846.

A second exhibit is located on the grounds of the Van Buren County Court House in Keosauqua. It honors the contribution of William Pitt's Brass Band to the emigrating Saints. The band, originally formed in Nauvoo, accompanied the settlers who traveled with Brigham Young and was an immeasurable source of strength and comfort. Pioneer journals record that whenever the spirits of the party were down, the band would start playing, and the pioneers would start singing.

The band was also a source of revenue for the Saints. In Van Buren

County, the inhabitants of Farmington and Keosauqua requested the band play for their communities in exchange for pay. They were so well-received at Keosauqua that they played three nightly performances. Their concerts were received in a crowded room in the Keosauqua courthouse, which is the oldest continuously used courthouse in Iowa.

The illustration on the exhibit and at the end of this chapter shows members of the band in costume playing in the pioneer camp. One journal account records that Brigham Young had been ill and members of the band played for him outside his tent to give comfort and support.

## PIONEER CAMPS IN VAN BUREN COUNTY

*Reed's Creek camp* (March 3–4). Ten acres were cleared by Bishop Miller and the pioneers for this camp east of the town of Bonaparte.

*Indian Creek camp* (March 5–6). This campsite is at the north end of the recently created Lake Sugema, an outdoor recreation reservoir on Indian Creek.

*Richardson's Point* (March 7–18). This campsite is west of Keosauqua along county road J40 and almost to the county border. Signs mark the spot where the Saints stayed several days. From here, Pitt's Brass Band made three trips to the courthouse in Keosauqua to give concerts and raise money for their journey.

## OTHER SITES OF INTEREST IN VAN BUREN COUNTY

*Bonaparte.* This was a flourishing town in 1846. The rocky river bed provided a crossing for the pioneer wagons. The park along the river where the wayside exhibit is located offers a grand view of the Des Moines River at this point.

*Bentonsport.* An old river town that is in a lovely and picturesque setting. Many buildings stem from the 1840s and bear a remarkable resemblance to those at Nauvoo. It is believed that Mason House Inn was built by the Mormons in exchange for goods.

*Keosauqua.* The oldest standing courthouse in Iowa is on a hill in this county seat and was the site of the Pitt's Brass Band concerts.

*Lacey-Keosauqua State Park.* Camping and other recreational facilities are available.

## DIRECTIONS TO INTERPRETIVE PANELS
## IN VAN BUREN COUNTY

1. County Road J40 goes through Bonaparte. The panel is in Riverfront Park and looks out toward the river crossing site.
2. Take Highway 1 into Keosauqua. The courthouse is in the northern portion of town. It has been restored and is open to the public. Parking is behind the courthouse, and the panel is behind the building, near the parking area.

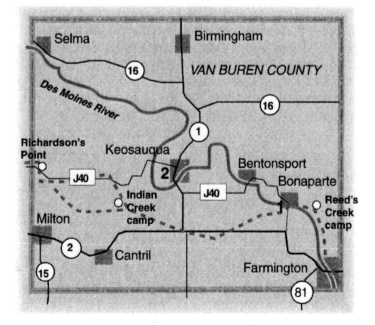

# DAVIS COUNTY
*Working Toward Zion*

The industry that built Nauvoo was also put to use as the Saints began their trek west. Many families began the trip without enough means or supplies to last the duration of the journey. Wherever they could, the pioneer men spread throughout the surrounding area and worked odd jobs. They were paid money and supplies that aided their journey. They cleared land, cut rails for fences, cut and hewed logs for cabins and in some cases built cabins for local settlers. The Mormons could complete a cabin in a day. Some of their craftsmanship can be seen in buildings that still stand.

A wayside exhibit is located near the Davis County Historical Museum in Bloomfield. The museum, housed in an Italianate home southeast of the town square, features a restored 1846 cabin constructed with logs hewn by the Mormons. The drawing on the exhibit shown at the beginning of this chapter illustrates activities associated with cutting, splitting and shaping lumber to be used for building. Mormon craftsmen not only earned support for the trek but left a legacy of workmanship in the communities they passed through.

Pioneer cabin, Bloomfield, Illinois

The second interpretive panel in Davis County is located at Drakesville Park on the western side of the town of Drakesville. Another cabin built by the pioneers in 1846 is located here. This is also the point where the original Mormon Trail veers south. Brigham Young and the advanced camp stayed near the Missouri border and settlements where they felt the Saints could trade for food and grain. But because of weather and terrain, travel along the southern route proved such a hardship in the spring of 1846 that later companies were advised to find a more northerly route.

The illustration on the wayside exhibit depicts the moment when John Gleason, dispatched from Brigham Young's camp, directed the companies to abandon the original route and follow the high ridges to the north.

### PIONEER CAMPS IN DAVIS COUNTY

*Evans camp* (March 19). The Saints camped here in a timbered area owned by a Widow Evans. The area is a few miles northeast of Bloomfield, the county seat.

*Davis County camp* (March 20). This site is southwest of Drakesville, almost to Highway 2, on the south side of the Fox River.

## OTHER SITES OF INTEREST IN DAVIS COUNTY

*West Grove.* This town along Highway 2 is on the prairie ridge the Saints had used in 1838–1839 while fleeing from Missouri to Illinois.

*Lake Wapello State Park.* Includes camping and visitor facilities.

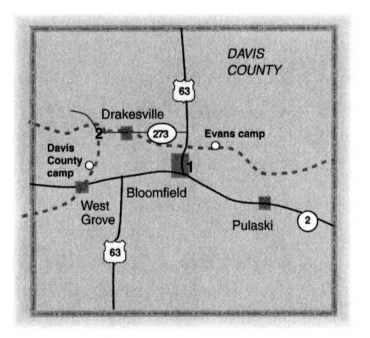

## DIRECTIONS TO INTERPRETIVE PANELS IN DAVIS COUNTY

1. The exhibit is located at the historical museum complex southeast of the town square in Bloomfield.

2. The wayside exhibit is in Drakesville Park, about four miles west of U.S. Highway 63. A cabin built by the pioneers in 1846 is also located here.

# APPANOOSE COUNTY

## A River Crossing and a Baby

The pioneers entered southeastern Appanoose County and camped near the town of Moulton on March 21, 1846. Heading west toward the Chariton River, the trail crossed a large floodplain. It is easy to imagine the hardship wagons would have faced traveling across this area during a heavy spring thunderstorm.

After the Saints reached and crossed the rising Chariton River, they camped on a ridge out of the floodplain and, because of inclement weather, stayed at the camp for 10 days.

The river crossing at the Chariton proved to be considerably difficult. The banks were steep on either side, and the Saints used ropes as brakes for the wagons being let down the hill on the east bank and to help pull the oxen up the west bank.

The company took the entire day of March 22 to cross the river. William Clayton recorded in his journal that he spent the whole time helping the teams and at the end of the day was so sore and tired that he could hardly walk.

The current channel of the river is different than in 1846; it was straightened and relocated in 1906 to help with flood control.

Wagon train reenactment at Chariton River camp, 1996

An interpretive panel marks the site of the actual crossing. Wagon ruts can be clearly seen on the hill from the campsite down to the crossing. Three graves are also marked in the area. The drawing on the exhibit at the beginning of this chapter shows men using ropes to assist the oxen up the banks. Most likely more than one team of oxen were hooked to the wagons.

During the Chariton crossing, Zina D. Huntington Jacobs gave birth to a boy. Though the circumstance of the birth was extremely stressful, she was so grateful the baby was born healthy that she named him Chariton in honor of the place.

In 1996, as part of a sesquicentennial reenactment of the pioneer wagon train, a Sunday memorial service was held at the Chariton campsite. A grandson of Chariton Jacobs was in attendance.

The second wayside exhibit in Appanoose County shown as the last illustration in this chapter is located on the northeast side of Lake Rathbun. Another crossing of the Chariton River, along the northern route of the trail, was near this site. As the Saints wound across the prairie, the travelers resembled, according to one pioneer journal entry, the movement of a great nation. The drawing on this interpretive panel represents what that might have looked like.

## Pioneer Camps in Appanoose County

*Coffman's camp* (March 21). This campsite is just west of present-day Moulton, on the north side of Locust Creek.

*Chariton River camp* (March 22–31). This site is about a mile west of the Chariton River because of a change in the river channel. Follow the small road signs marked "historical site."

*Shoal Creek camp* (April 1–2). This campsite is southwest of the town of Exline, west of Shoal Creek.

## Other Sites of Interest in Appanoose County

*Lake Rathbun.* Boating, camping, bike trails and other facilities are available.

*Iconium.* A pioneer camp was on the northern portion of the trail, northeast of Iconium. Some wintered there at a large spring in the area.

## DIRECTIONS TO INTERPRETIVE PANELS
## IN APPANOOSE COUNTY

1. The Chariton River crossing is more difficult to find but
   worth the search. Out of Exline Junction, follow County
   Road T-30 south. Keep following the historical marker signs
   that direct you to the site. You must travel quite a distance to
   reach the site.

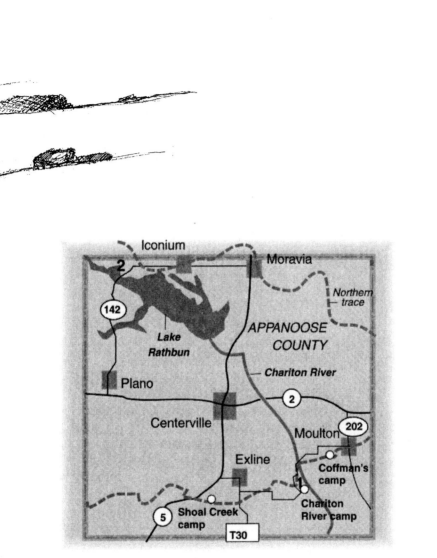

2. From State Highway 5 take Highway 142 west to the Bridgeview area adjacent to Rathbun Lake. The northern route of the trail went past the south side of the Milledgeville cemetery. Wagon ruts can still be seen on a high hill overlooking Lake Rathbun.

# WAYNE COUNTY

*The Hymn Heard Around the World*

Two significant encampments of the Saints occurred southeast of the town of Corydon. Rain had fallen incessantly in the spring of 1846 and wagon-breaking, animal-stopping and human-clinging black mud was a constant obstacle to travel. The area where the trail passed through Wayne County is a succession of low hills cut by creek drainages. Because of weather conditions and topography, the wagons kept as much as possible to the ridge tops, "wending" their way, back and forth, across the southern Iowa prairie.

The two campsites were a short distance apart, along Locust Creek. Locust Creek camp 1 was on a broad ridge on the Middle Fork of Locust Creek. The Saints camped here, halted by the rain for a week. On April 6, they celebrated the 16th anniversary of the founding of the church. There Brigham Young noted the condition of the emigrants and decided to find a site for a semipermanent settlement to assist weary Saints who needed rest and additional preparation before resuming the rigors of the trail. Garden Grove would become that settlement.

On April 13, the camp moved one-half mile (an indication of the muddy conditions) down the ridge to Locust Creek camp 2. Provisions were running low, and there was no forage for hungry horses and cattle. The next day, William Clayton remarked in his diary that they were "blockaded by mud." After spending a miserable night protecting the camp's provisions from hungry animals, he received the glad news that his son had been born in Nauvoo. Clayton sat down and composed the hymn "All Is Well." It is a message that acknowledges hardships but inspires perseverance and affirms the triumph of faith.

Later named "Come, Come Ye Saints," the song became the anthem of a people, encouraging not only the pioneers of 1846 but their spiritual descendents as well. According to Loren Horton, former senior historian for the State Historical Society of Iowa, it was the first song ever written in the state.

Wayne County historian D. Elbert Pidcock spent years researching the exact route of the trail through the county and has located the Locust Creek campsites. The Mormon Church has placed a plaque in honor of the hymn in front of the Tharp Cemetery, a short distance north of campsite 2.

The illustration on the interpretive panel at this site and at this chapter's beginning shows William Clayton, Diantha (his fourth wife), and new son. The lyrics and music of "Come, Come Ye Saints" are as

Tharp Cemetery, near site where William Clayton wrote "Come, Come Ye Saints"

inspiring today as they were then, and the drawing of two women and two boys singing the hymn could be from any time period.

To honor the Mormon pioneers, *Des Moines Register* columnist Chuck Offenburger encouraged hundreds of congregations of all denominations across Iowa to sing "Come, Come Ye Saints" as part of their worship services on the anniversary of the song's composition in 1996.

A second interpretive panel is located on the grounds of the Wayne County Historical Museum (which also has an exhibit honoring the Mormon pioneers) on the eastern edge of Corydon. This wayside exhibit is dedicated to the sacrifice and work of women along the trail.

The illustration, the last in this chapter, shows a typical campsite and women engaged in the daily activities of preparing food and taking care of children. The domestic needs of the emigrant Saints were constant and primarily the responsibility of women. They baked bread, cooked meals and administered to the sick. They prepared the dead for burial and gave birth—sometimes in ice storms with no shelter except pots and pans held over them by other women, sometimes on the banks of rivers they were just about to ford or had just crossed. They kept up studies for the children and wrote in journals.

The true and often unsung heroes of the Mormon expedition were its women. They sacrificed comfortable homes, gave up the security and privacy of their own hearths and extended themselves selflessly to the service of others. They continued the care of family and belongings when husbands and sons were called to serve in the Mormon Battalion, sent on missions or participated in other expeditions. Many women gave their own lives or continued on the trail alone after their husbands or children had died next to them or, worse, did not return from expeditions away from the family.

### PIONEER CAMPS IN WAYNE COUNTY

*Hickory Grove camp* (April 3–6). This camp was the first stopping point inside Wayne County. Because of mud and wooded terrain, the wagons were not able to travel far each day. There were more campsites in Wayne County than any other Iowa county.

*Locust Creek camp 1* (April 7–12). The Locust Creek campsites are not far from one another. They are southwest of the town of Seymour.

*Locust Creek camp 2* (April 13–15). This campsite is a little south of Tharp Cemetery, where the exhibit honoring the writing of "Come, Come Ye Saints" stands.

*Rolling Prairie camp* (April 16). This campsite is just north of County Road J46.

*Pleasant Point camp* (April 17–20). The Saints followed an existing road out of Rolling Prairie camp but, after realizing it would take them into Missouri, left it and turned north. They camped just southeast of the town of Allerton.

*Camp Creek camp* (April 21). The wagons traveled to a point just northwest of Allerton.

*Pleasant Grove camp* (April 22). This campsite and Muddy Creek campsite are near one another on the western edge of Wayne County.

*Muddy Creek camp* (April 23).

## OTHER SITES OF INTEREST IN WAYNE COUNTY

*Allerton.* "The Inn of the Six-Toed Cat," a hotel built in the 1800s, and an apiary to raise bees to produce honey are on the main street of this small town. East of Allerton is a restored round barn.

*Corydon.* The county seat of Wayne County and home to the Wayne County Museum, which has a Mormon Trail display, including a three-quarter replica of oxen and wagons traveling through the Iowa mud. Corydon Lake and Park are on the southwest side of town.

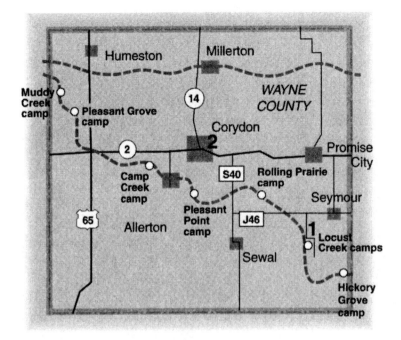

## Directions to Interpretive Panels
## in Wayne County

1. To find Tharp Cemetery, take County Road J46 west of Seymour. Turn south on 210th and proceed 2.7 miles on the gravel road to the cemetery on the east side of the road.
2. The other exhibit is located outside the Prairie Trails Museum on the east edge of Corydon on Highway 2.

# LUCAS COUNTY
*Traveling Prairie Ridges*

The northern trace of the Mormon Trail crosses what is now Lucas County, the only county that does not include a portion of the "official" trail as well. The southern route that Brigham Young's pioneer party followed was abandoned in favor of a more easily navigable path.

The total Mormon contribution to the westward movement during a several-year period included about 70,000 emigrants. Most of those followed the northern trace. At times, the trail was heavy with wagon traffic. Early Lucas County settlers claimed seeing 100 to 200 wagons a day during peak traveling times.

Newel Knight recalled, "After travelling a short distance we found ourselves on the broad and extensive Prairie. Here we could look forward for miles and behold the Prairie spotted with wagons Cattle horses and sheep, Men, Women and Children who all seemed to be in good Spirits."

The Mormons were not traveling west as explorers or adventurers. They didn't blaze their own trails unless they had to, instead following roads and paths of those who had preceded them across the prairie. In Iowa, those roads were sometimes of poor quality, and in such cases the Saints worked to make them better for those who followed. The trail generally followed high ridges because they were well drained and faster to traverse than the muddy creek bottoms. It often followed the same paths used by buffaloes and Indians.

Both interpretive panels in Lucas County are in the county seat of

Chariton. The first, seen in the beginning of this chapter, includes a drawing representing a wagon train wending its way across a grassy ridge.

The second panel, on the courthouse lawn in Chariton, depicts the scene of a trail tragedy, a wagon accident that killed Sarah Gabbut in October of 1846 (see chapter's end). After crossing the Chariton River, Sarah attempted to get back into her wagon, but the churn she grabbed to help her climb in gave way and she fell. Startled, the oxen ran and the heavy wagon rolled over Sarah's abdomen. Thomas Bullock wrote, "She exclaimed 'Oh dear, I am dying.' She lingered until 5 minutes to 1 and breathed her last. ... We continued over hill and dale until we came to one of the tributaries of 'White Breast.' ... Laid Sister Gabbut out in her robes, and prepared a grave."

Accidents with wagons and animals were common on the trail. Most were not fatal. But this tragedy and the many injuries that did occur remind us that the pioneers were subject to the typical experiences of all those who traveled westward. They suffered accidents, disease, cold, hunger, hard labor and failure of equipment. They also experienced the typical challenges of personal relationships—between family members and those living close to one another because of the demands of travel together.

## PIONEER CAMPS IN LUCAS COUNTY

This county is the only trail county that contains a portion of the northern trace of the Mormon Trail but no portions of the southern route.

## OTHER SITES OF INTEREST IN LUCAS COUNTY

*Grave Hollow.* This area was a campsite and the burial site of Sarah Gabbut (see county map).

*Chariton.* This is the county seat of Lucas County and home of Lucas County Historical Museum.

*Red Haw State Park.* A beautiful state park with many facilities.

*Stephen's State Forest.* Includes a campground, picnic area and horseback riding.

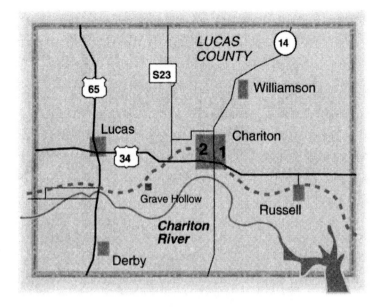

## DIRECTIONS TO INTERPRETIVE PANELS IN LUCAS COUNTY

1. Both exhibits are in the town of Chariton. The first is on the frontage road on the north side of Highway 34, just to the east of Highway 14.
2. The second exhibit is on the courthouse lawn in Chariton.

# DECATUR COUNTY
## The Magic City of the Woods

On April 24, Orson Pratt wrote, "We came to a place we named Garden Grove. At this point we determined to form a small settlement and open farms for the benefit of the poor, and such as are unable to pursue their journey further, and also for the benefit of the poor who were yet behind." The location was approximately the halfway mark in the Saints' journey across Iowa.

A few days later, Hosea Stout arrived and noted that so quickly had the settlement grown it seemed to appear like a "Magic City of the Woods."

The development of the Garden Grove settlement revealed the organization and industry of the traveling Saints. Labor was divided and organized according to need. Some 100 men were assigned to cut trees, split rails, put up fences and cut logs. Forty-eight men began building houses. Twelve men dug wells, and 20 built bridges on the Grand River. The remainder began to plow, harrow and plant grain. Within a couple of weeks, the workers had cleared and fenced two farms, built houses and bridges and left a surplus of 10,000 rails for future use and enough logs for 30 or 40 additional houses.

There were two housing sites of interesting construction established for those who would stay at Garden Grove. One site consisted of a string of log houses, about 60 structures, arranged close to one another in checkerboard fashion. Most of the cabins were duplexes and

Garden Grove site

included fireplaces made of clay—a luxury greatly appreciated by the inhabitants. The second site consisted of approximately 20 structures.

The site today indicates how the cabins were laid out in the settlement, according to Paul and Karla Gunzenhauser, owners of the settlement site. The Gunzenhausers were a key force in preserving and developing the site at Garden Grove and encouraging preservation all along the trail in southern Iowa.

The illustrations of both panels at the settlement site reflect what might have been observed at the time of its occupancy. One, this chapter's opening, shows the industry of building rail fences and suggests the communal nature of the settlement's lifestyle with a large cooking pot in the foreground. The other, at the end of this chapter, depicts the log cabins placed close together in rows that were typical of the structures built at Garden Grove.

Here was respite from the rigors of the trail. Many of the poorest of the Saints, who had no means to continue onward, stayed, rested and rebuilt their supplies. For some, Garden Grove became a final resting place, and those who died were buried in a small cemetery in a wooded area just west of the settlement. For others, the community was a short respite before they continued on to camps on the Missouri River.

Garden Grove cemetery and monument

A little to the north of the settlement site is a park that includes a picnic shelter. The Church of Jesus Christ of Latter-day Saints erected a granite monument there just west of what is believed to be the site of the pioneer cemetery.

Garden Grove is a town proud of its pioneer heritage. It is home to the Mormon Trail schools and the high school mascot is the Saints. A small marker commemorating the founding of the community by Mormon pioneers was placed in the town park by Ezra Taft Benson, whose grandfather was born here in 1846.

### PIONEER CAMPS IN DECATUR COUNTY

*Garden Grove* (April 24–May 12). The settlement site is worth spending a little extra time. It is a beautiful site and well marked.

*Hickory Thunder camp* (May 13–14). This camp received its name from a heavy thunderstorm that struck the company while it was in this area of the county.

### OTHER SITES IN DECATUR COUNTY

*Garden Grove.* In the town park a small marker commemorates the founding of the community by the pioneers in 1846. The town is home

Mormon Trail High School, Garden Grove. School mascot: the Saints

of the Mormon Trail school district. The McClung House is available for overnight lodging.

*Trailside Historical Park.* The park is in walking distance north of the settlement site. A memorial marks the burial ground of the Saints.

*Lamoni.* Home to Graceland College, owned by the Reorganized Church of Jesus Christ of Latter Day Saints. Liberty Hall, a home of Joseph Smith III, son of Joseph Smith Jr., has been restored and is open to visitors. The town also has many antique shops.

*Nine Eagles State Park.* Located in the south-central part of the county.

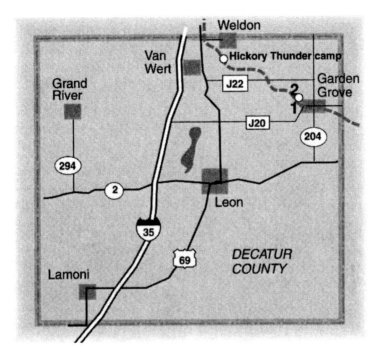

## DIRECTIONS TO INTERPRETIVE PANELS
## IN DECATUR COUNTY

> 1, 2. Both exhibits are at the settlement site north of Garden Grove. Go west of town about one-half mile. Turn right off the curve and travel on the gravel road another one-half mile. Signs clearly mark the way.

# CLARKE COUNTY
*Travel—Different Means, Same Path*

Through the eastern half of Iowa, the Mormon migration followed existing roads as much as possible and stayed near settlements where the pioneers could work for pay and goods that would help them in their travels. Across the western half of Iowa, where settlements were more scattered, they often blazed new trails and built new roads and bridges.

However, the route they followed was not entirely untraveled. It generally followed Indian paths and the course of previously migrating buffalo. These animals also sought the most convenient way across the uninhabited prairie.

The interpretive panel in the town of Murray, Iowa, explains this progression of travel. The Mormon wagons that followed the buffaloes' path were in turn followed by stagecoaches and other migrating travelers. And finally, the route chosen by the railroads often followed the same course.

Pioneer cabin at Murray

Thomas Bullock recorded in 1846, "We crossed several bad hollows, walked in the Indian trail and we encamped about 7:00 on the Prairie."

The southern and northern parts of the Mormon Trail come together in Clarke County, the southern trail leading from Garden Grove to Mt. Pisgah.

Many campsites and portions of the trail have been identified thanks to a community service grant from the Iowa Department of Education given to the Murray Community School. In 1994 and 1995, two groups of students, receiving high school credit for their work, searched land throughout the county and made significant finds. Wagon ruts can be seen two miles west of Murray.

Another panel exists next to the Clarke County Historical Museum, just south of Osceola. The exhibit recounts the experience of a lost camp of families who wintered by themselves in this area, separate from the main body of wagons. They were young families, with small children. The illustration, seen at the end of this chapter, shows a lone, blanketed figure facing a fire in a winter camp and depicts the extremes of the Iowa winter. The dilemma of the lost families and the hardship of their experience is a poignant story. One family of four children came down with chills and fever. Clarence Merrill, one of the children, recorded: "We live in a one room log house, four of us children came down with chills and fever. They buried my brother Alonzo then the baby."

Students from the Murray School located and mapped the old camp and noted the remains of two dugouts, both five feet deep.

## PIONEER CAMPS IN CLARKE COUNTY

*Willow Bridge camp* (May 14). The pioneers dried out from a heavy rain.

*White Breast Creek* (May 15). This campsite is southwest of Osceola and a couple of miles northwest of the junction of the original trail and the northern trace.

*Long Creek camp* (May 16). The site is adjacent to Long Creek, just south of the town of Murray.

*Sevenmile Creek camp* (May 17). The campsite is east of Sevenmile Creek, just north of Highway 34.

## OTHER SITES OF INTEREST IN CLARKE COUNTY

*Osceola.* This town is the county seat of Clarke County. The Clarke County Historical Museum includes exhibits on the history and heritage of southern Iowa. A Mormon chapel is east of town on the north side of Highway 34.

*Murray.* Ruts from the original trail can be seen west of town. From the interpretive panel and cabin, follow the road parallel to the railroad tracks two miles west out of Murray and then one-fourth mile south. A platform, from which you can see the ruts in the field, is to the east of the road.

On January 28, 2000, four Mormon missionaries and one Murray man was killed in a tragic automobile accident on Highway 34 near the town of Murray. It was the greatest loss of missionary life in Mormon church history. Ironically the accident happened on the Mormon Trail. Killed were elders Jaysen Christiansen, Jared Pulham, Daniel Roundy and Bradly Savage, all of Utah, and Herman Heckathorn of Murray.

## DIRECTIONS TO INTERPRETIVE PANELS IN CLARKE COUNTY

1. The first wayside exhibit is adjacent to the parking lot of the Clarke County Historical Museum. The museum is just south of Osceola on the west side of Highway 69.

2. The second exhibit is in the town of Murray. Turn north off Highway 34 and go to the north end of Murray. The panel is next to a log cabin across from the railroad tracks.

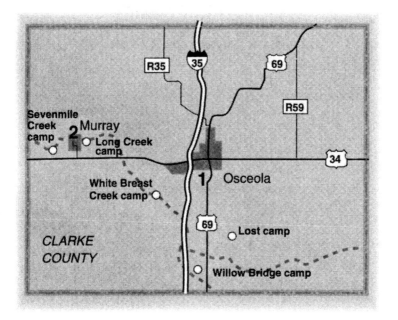

# UNION COUNTY

*A Second Permanent Settlement*

Not long after a permanent encampment was established at Garden Grove, Parley P. Pratt was sent to find a site for a second settlement. On May 18, impressed by the beautiful vista of the Grand River valley and an abundance of wildlife, he named the location Mt. Pisgah after the place where Moses had first viewed the promised land. His autobiography states, "Being pleased and excited at the varied beauty before me, I cried out, 'This is Mt. Pisgah.'" The promised land was still far from this modern camp of Israel, but Pratt's expression was an indication of vision, hope and faith.

Work began immediately, with the same industry and organization as was shown at Garden Grove, and four days after they arrived, the Saints had cleaned, plowed, fenced and seeded 1,000 acres. Dugouts were constructed for immediate shelter, cabins begun and the wagons rolled in. At various times, Mt. Pisgah was home to 3,000 to 5,000 people.

The site was one of sadness as well as hope and rest. Many of the travelers, weary from the slow and difficult journey across southern Iowa and suffering malnutrition from limited provisions, became ill (mostly with scurvy) and died, including scores of children. Deaths in the first few months were estimated between 160 and 300. In total as many as 800 Saints were buried at Mt. Pisgah. The estimates are vague because so

Mt. Pisgah monument and cemetery

many died, so fast, that keeping accurate records was impossible.

In 1888, the Mormon Church purchased two acres of land and erected a monument to those who had died at Mt. Pisgah.

Later, Union County purchased several more acres around this site and established a park. In 1996, as part of the sesquicentennial celebration of the trail in Iowa, Des Moines anesthesiologist Ray Ritzman directed members of the Des Moines, Iowa, Stake (a group of several Mormon congregations) in building a replica cabin on the site.

Mt. Pisgah is unique because of the abundance of artifacts and remnants of the trail still visible. Impressions remain of dugouts built in an embankment where the center of the settlement was located south of the county park. Wheel ruts are easily seen on the hills just east of the Mt. Pisgah monument. Bob Brown, the farmer who owns the Mt. Pisgah land, has restored an old schoolhouse to serve as a visitors center for the area. For the past several years, local schoolchildren aided by a grant from the state of Iowa have helped him study and identify historical locations.

The illustration at the interpretive panel at Mt. Pisgah captures two men building a type of fence pioneers in 1846 might have built, with a

Dedication of the Mt. Pisgah cabin, 1996

dugout represented in the middle ground and a team of horses plowing a field in the background near a bank of trees (see chapter opening illustration). Despite weariness, illness and death, Mt. Pisgah was a place of industry and preparation—a momentary stopping place on the way to a permanent home.

A second Union County panel is located at Threemile Lake. This reservoir in the central part of the county has as its source Threemile Creek. The trail traveled west about where the reservoir's dam presently is. The creeks and rivers in this area apparently had no names when the Mormons lived here, so the pioneers named them based on how far away they were from Mt. Pisgah. The drawing on the wayside exhibit, included at the end of this chapter, shows wagons crossing a stream on the prairie.

Grand River valley from the Mt. Pisgah cabin, 1996

Eliza R. Snow recorded in August of 1846, "We expected to have started this mor[ning], but br. M[arkham]'s oxen stray'd & we were only able to go 3 m[ile]s across the river."

## PIONEER CAMPS IN UNION COUNTY

*Mt. Pisgah* (May 18–June 1). The site of the second semipermanent settlement is located east of the Grand River. The Saints first arrived in May, but as others came to the area, Mt. Pisgah became a group of settlements.

*Grand River camp* (June 2). Brigham Young's camp left Mt. Pisgah and, after traveling about four miles, made camp near Twomile Creek.

*Twelvemile Creek camp* (June 3). This site is located about a mile east of Twelvemile Creek.

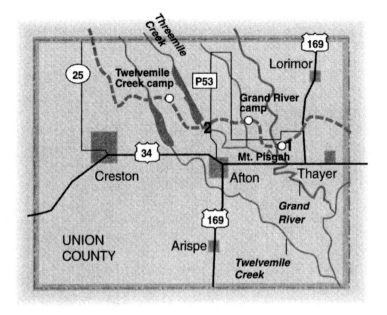

## OTHER SITES OF INTEREST IN UNION COUNTY

*Creston.* This southern Iowa town has restaurants, parks and lodging. There is a visitors center in an old Phillips 66 station on the west edge of town, a Union County historical complex in McKinley Park and a county courthouse.

*Green Valley State Park.* An Iowa state park with camping and other outdoor activities. There is a general trail sign here as well.

*Afton.* The town of Afton was the county seat in the late 1800s. Garfield Park has been used for more than 100 years.

## DIRECTIONS TO INTERPRETIVE PANELS IN UNION COUNTY

1. The first wayside exhibit is at Mt. Pisgah. From Highway 34, turn north on Highway 169 and go two miles. Turn west on a dirt road. Signs direct you to the park and cemetery. You will pass through a farmer's yard just before you arrive.

2. The second panel is at the campground overlooking Threemile Lake. Take county road P53 north out of Afton; then travel west on H33 to the campground.

# ADAIR COUNTY
## An Easier Trail Across Iowa Prairie

As the Saints crossed the area that is now Adair County, they traversed much undisturbed Iowa prairie. Prairie originally covered some 80 percent of the state. Today, relics of tallgrass prairie are restricted to small tracts and comprise less than 2 percent of Iowa's land.

Early settlement in Iowa proceeded from the southeast, along rivers and tributaries, to the northwestern part of the state. Prairie grasslands were often last to be cultivated by settlers. They were open and caused uneasiness in settlers coming from eastern woodlands. They were also short on water and fuel. Not until after the Mormon migration was the rich bounty of Iowa's prairie soil fully appreciated. As the pioneers moved toward their Zion in the Great Basin of the American West, they crossed some of the richest agricultural soil in the world.

In 1846, the occupants of the slow-moving wagon trains enjoyed relative ease of travel across the prairie in the western portion of the state. The vanguard of the exodus crossed these lands in late spring and early summer. Behind them were the rushing tributaries swollen with spring rains. Behind were the muddy roads and timbered drainages. They traveled more distance in a day and could enjoy the beauty that surrounded them.

The tallgrass prairie contained much that was beautiful. Switchgrass, big bluestem, lead plant and coneflowers were typical species. The bright magenta of downy phlox and the delicate pink blooms of native wild roses were delightful discoveries for the travelers.

Pioneer children were most able to enjoy the treasures of the prairie. As they walked alongside the wagons and beside the livestock, they had time to observe and enjoy the native plant life. On the prairie, where the wagon train could be seen for long distances, children often ran ahead and played games until the wagons caught up with them.

Children on the trail were given responsibilities to assist their families. They helped gather fuel, cook meals, watch livestock and take care of other siblings. Early journals of the trek across Iowa rarely mention children and their activities. Newel Knight wrote, "Our children amuse themselves with the sweet and beautiful flowers which grow spontaneous."

However, many children wrote their recollections later in life. Sarah Sophia Moulding wrote about her memories of traveling as a 3-year-old, "As little as I was, I can remember the noise of the wagon and

Trail ruts near Mormon Trail Park

Sign at ruts near Mormon Trail Park

the jingle-jangle of the pots and kettles fastened underneath and at the sides of the wagon."

The interpretive panel at the historical museum in the center of the town of Orient focuses on children growing up on the trail. The drawing, seen at the end of this chapter, indicates activities that might have been typical of a child's day on the trek. The "Bank of Memories" display at the museum features a Mormon exhibit.

An interpretive panel also exists at the Mormon Trail Park southeast of Bridgewater. The drawing, seen at the beginning of this chapter, focuses on the native plants and wildlife that the wagons would have passed crossing the area. Well-defined wagon ruts are evident east of the park, and an area of reconstructed prairie shows what the pioneers would have seen in 1846.

## PIONEER CAMPS IN ADAIR COUNTY

*Bromberry Hill camp* (June 4). This campsite is a couple of miles west of the town of Orient.

*Shoal or Small Creek camp* (June 5). This campsite is south of Bridgewater on the banks of the west branch of the Middle Nodaway River.

## OTHER SITES OF INTEREST IN ADAIR COUNTY

*Greenfield.* The county seat has a renovated courthouse as the centerpiece of the town square. The Adair County historical complex has exhibits about life in the early days of settlement in Iowa. Lake Greenfield, southwest of town, has fishing, sailing and trail facilities, but no camping. Lake Nodaway has camping, showers and fishing.

*Mormon Trail Park.* This park southeast of Bridgewater is beautiful, with excellent camping facilities.

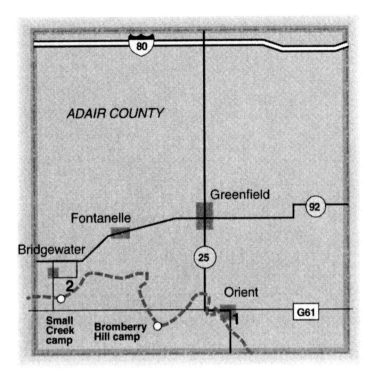

An Easier Trail Across Iowa Prairie

## DIRECTIONS TO INTERPRETIVE PANELS IN ADAIR COUNTY

1. The first wayside exhibit is in the town of Orient. Highway 25 goes through the town, and the Bank of Memories is located in the center of the community.

2. The second exhibit is at Mormon Trail Park. Just south of Bridgewater, follow the signs two miles east to the park. Once in the park, historical marker signs lead to the right and direct you to the panel. Directions to nearby trail ruts are at the exhibit area.

**71**

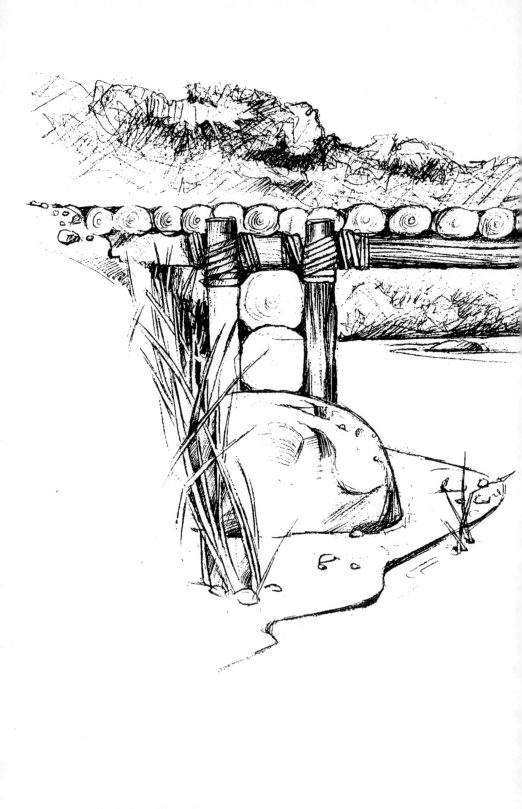

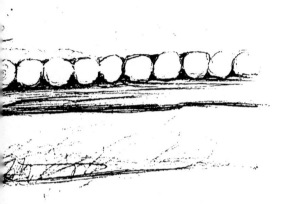

# Cass County

*Building Bridges and Meeting Indians*

The Mormon trek across Iowa was often difficult, fraught with struggle and sometimes tragedy. The cold and ice of Iowa's winter and early spring were extreme. Deep muddy roads saturated by heavy thunderstorms hindered and sometimes halted the movement of wagons, livestock and pioneers. Inadequate supplies, illness and exhaustion took their toll.

But the Saints and their leaders responded to the trials of the Iowa journey with resolution and ingenuity. The struggles united them, in purpose and organization. When a chosen route was too difficult, they found another. When travelers were too sick or unprepared to travel, they established temporary settlements, planted crops and built homes to help with recuperation and preparation. When organization and communication broke down, they formed companies of 10s, 50s and 100s.

Iowa was the great proving ground for the Mormon migration. Here, the pioneers focused on and refined their purpose and process.

Their struggles and accomplishments while crossing the land between the mighty Mississippi and the wide Missouri make the Iowa Mormon Trail a great unpolished jewel in the legacy of the Saints' trek west.

In 1846 no direct and continuous trail was across the state. In some areas the Mormons were able to follow existing trails. In others they connected those fragments with roads of their own making. When no pretraveled roads were available, trailblazers picked the best routes and cleared the way.

The trailblazing through Iowa included constant bridge building. The pioneers built structures wherever they could across Iowa's many streams and rivers. Where they couldn't, they built ferries. Some bridges were hastily constructed and lasted only a short time. They had to be rebuilt by following companies. Others were strong enough that, as Col. Thomas Kane, a friend of the Mormons from Philadelphia, put it, "They were capable of carrying heavy artillery."

Because of the many stream crossings the journey required, the bridges Mormon pioneers built aided the travel of the many emigrants who followed them. According to journal reports, when a bridge was needed a squad of men was detailed for the task. The bridges helped tie together bits and pieces of a trail into a wagon route. The interpretive panel in Lyman (at the intersection of highways 71 and 92) illustrates how a pioneer bridge might have looked (see chapter opening).

The nickname Mormon comes from the religion's acceptance of the Book of Mormon as a second volume of Holy Scripture. The Bible is a record of the peoples in ancient Israel. The Book of Mormon is a record of the ancient inhabitants of the Western Hemisphere. It includes the story of ancestors of the American Indian, whom the book refers to as Lamanites, named after a founding father.

In Cass County, many Mormons met Lamanites for the first time. The Pottawattamie Indians had temporarily settled in southwest Iowa about the time the Mormons fled Missouri and began to settle Nauvoo. Near the crossing of the Nishnabotna River, the wagon trail passed by a Pottawattamie village. The Saints bartered with the Indians and held friendly discussions with them.

Nishnabotna Ferry House

An interpretive panel is located on the grounds of the Hitchcock House in the town of Lewis. The exhibit overlooks the point where Brigham Young crossed the Nishnabotna and passed by the Indian village. The drawing indicates the friendly nature of the meeting and shows the style of the Pottawattamie wigwams, which numbered about a hundred.

Near the Hitchcock House sits the Nishnabotna Ferry House. The building is no longer on the river's edge because the channel was straightened in the 1920s, but thousands of pioneers crossed the river here as they migrated westward.

A wayside exhibit on the site honors the trek of the handcart pioneers. Though they traveled from Iowa City to Winter Quarters, the Mormon settlement on the Missouri River, and on to Salt Lake City 10 years and more after the migration of 1846, they used the same trail through western Iowa. The tales of the sacrifice and suffering of these foot travelers are among the most poignant in all the records of western migration in America. Though the handcart companies followed the original trek by 10 years, it is fitting that they are included as part of the Iowa Mormon Trail (see end of chapter illustration).

## Pioneer Camps in Cass County

*Nodaway River camp* (June 6). This campsite is on the West Nodaway River a few miles south of the town of Cumberland.

*Pleasant Prairie camp* (June 7). The camp moved to this site, which was considered safer because it was away from the Indian area.

## Other Sites of Interest in Cass County

*Atlantic.* This town is the county seat of Cass County.

*Lewis.* Several pioneer sites are near the town of Lewis—the Nishnabotna River crossing, old Indiantown (a couple of miles west of Lewis), Nishnabotna Ferry House and Hitchcock House.

*Cold Springs State Park.* This park includes camping facilities and electrical hookups.

*Lake Anita State Park.* This state park has camping areas, electrical hookups, showers and toilets.

## DIRECTIONS TO INTERPRETIVE PANELS IN CASS COUNTY

1. The first wayside exhibit is in the town of Lyman. The panel is on the southeast corner of highways 71 and 92.

2. The second exhibit in Cass County is at the Hitchcock House in the town of Lewis. Go west on Minnesota Street about 1

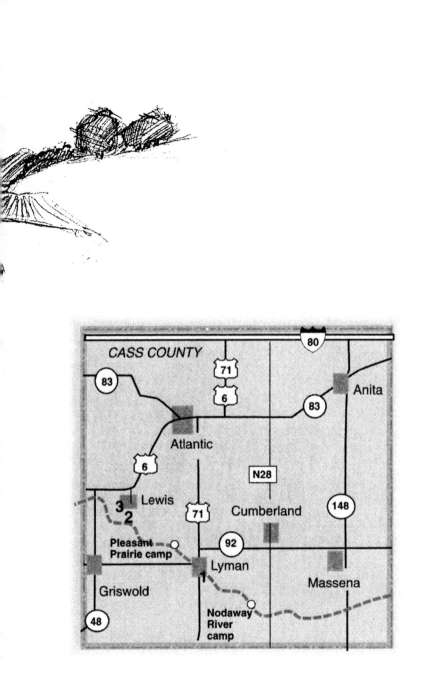

mile. At the sign go one-half mile to Hitchcock House.

3. The third exhibit is at the Nishnabotna Ferry House on the west edge of Lewis. Go west on Minnesota Street. It is on the north side of the street.

# POTTAWATTAMIE COUNTY
*The Grand Encampment*

Arrival in the Missouri River valley was cause to celebrate and rejoice. The first wagons reached the area in mid-June—four and a half months after crossing the Mississippi River and camping on Iowa soil. The Saints had taken as long to cross Iowa as they would to travel the remainder of the journey to the Great Basin.

By August it became clear the journey west could not be completed before winter, and a decision was made to settle for the season near the Missouri River. Thousands of Saints poured steadily into the region. In June and July they gathered at what was called the Grand Encampment, near where the Iowa School for the Deaf is now. Col. Thomas Kane recorded the most vivid description of what the camp looked like. He said the Council Bluff hills were "gay with bright white canvas, and alive with the busy stir of swarming occupants. In the clear blue morning air, the smoke streamed up from more than a thousand cooking fires." Kane observed that the only thing more numerous than the cattle were the children.

Forage for cattle and wood for fires became a primary concern of incoming wagon companies. After July, the gathering place changed

from one Grand Encampment to many temporary settlements up and down the Middle Missouri valley and on both sides of the river. Though the camps were scattered across a large area, the Mormon settlement of southwest Iowa and across the river into Nebraska can be viewed as one

unit. Wards and branches of the church were established. Cabins and other shelters were constructed. To tie the area and its settlers together and make quick communication possible, the Mormons went to work on ferries, roads and bridges that crisscrossed the region.

More than 80 original settlements were constructed from 1846 through 1853. Of those, nearly a dozen continued as permanent towns after the Mormon migration was completed. Personal and communal industry, betterment of present circumstances and assistance for those who would follow led the Saints to significant construction of roads and residences.

Their labors benefited more than the Mormon exodus. In 1846, they did not foresee the boon their personal labors would give the California gold rushers of 1849, an estimated 10,000 of whom also used the roads, bridges and ferries through the region on their way to hoped-for riches in the West.

The town of Macedonia in southern Pottawattamie County was originally settled by Mormon pioneers. They stayed there for a few years and even established a branch of the church. A wayside exhibit near a large red granite boulder marks the place where the trail approached the crossing of the West Nishnabotna River. The interpretive panel illustrates a wagon team crossing a bridge over the river. The Mormons moved on in 1852, leaving the hamlet to non-Mormon settlers.

Two interpretive signs are at the Iowa School for the Deaf. One celebrates the settlement of the many communities built by the Mormons in the middle Missouri valley. The illustration depicts the building of cabins on the Missouri River. Although the Mormons were planning on leaving for the west as soon as possible, they also wanted the comfort of safe shelter during the winter.

The other represents the site of the Grand Encampment (see chapter opening). The drawing indicates a scene Kane might have witnessed in July of 1846. The Grand Encampment was also the site of the mustering of the Mormon Battalion. Here 500 volunteers left their families to serve in the war between the United States and Mexico.

A fourth interpretive panel, seen at the end of this chapter, is placed near the reconstructed Kanesville Tabernacle at 222 East Broadway in Council Bluffs. The original tabernacle was the site where Brigham Young was sustained as second president of the Church of Jesus Christ of Latter-day Saints and official successor to Joseph Smith.

Reenacted mustering of the Mormon Battalion at the Grand Encampment site, 1996

### PIONEER CAMPS IN POTTAWATTAMIE COUNTY

*Pleasant Valley camp* (June 8). The pioneer camp entered Pottawattamie County and camped on the west side of Walnut Creek just south of present-day Highway 6.

*West Nishnabotna camp* (June 9–10). At this campsite near Macedonia, the group spent two nights while a bridge was built across the West Nishnabotna River.

*Silver Creek camp* (June 11). The Saints camped near Silver Creek.

*Keg Creek camp* (June 12). They camped near Keg Creek.

*Mosquito Creek camp* (June 13). This site overlooks the Missouri River. It was the first camp in Council Bluffs.

*Missouri River camp* (June 14). The group camped at the Missouri River.

Winter Quarters Visitors Center in Florence, Nebraska

## OTHER SITES OF INTEREST IN POTTAWATTAMIE COUNTY

*National Western Historic Center.* South of Interstate 80 on 24th Street South in Council Bluffs, this historic center commemorates the Mormon, Oregon, Lewis and Clark, and Pony Express trails.

*Lake Manawa State Park.* An Iowa state park with a large lake, hiking trails and camping sites.

*Winter Quarters.* A beautiful visitors center of the Church of Jesus Christ of Latter-day Saints looks across to the Winter Quarters cemetery. Tours are available every day. Turn south off Interstate 680 on Highway 75. Follow the signs to the visitors center.

*Council Bluffs and Omaha.* The metropolitan area offers complete services—restaurants, hotels, airport, art museum and zoo.

## Directions to Interpretive Panels in Pottawattamie County

1. In the town of Macedonia, one mile west of Highway 59, a wayside exhibit commemorates the bridge building and river crossing.

2 and 3. At the Grand Encampment site, located at the Iowa School for the Deaf, two panels commemorate the Saints in

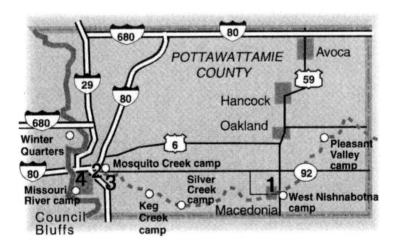

the Missouri River valley. Turn off Highway 92 onto Highway 275, and almost immediately turn left into the school campus. A marker commemorating the Mormon Battalion is also here.

4. Kanesville Tabernacle. The reconstructed building at 222 East Broadway, Council Bluffs, commemorates the sustaining of Brigham Young as second president of the Church of Jesus Christ of Latter-day Saints. The building contains exhibits and a gift shop.

# Conclusion
## A Legacy of Faith and Determination

The Iowa portion of the Mormon Trail is rich in its historical importance to the development of southern Iowa and westward migration in America. But more importantly, it is an example of the spiritual strength of those who traveled it. The legacy of their faith is an enduring gift to the generations following them—literally, historically and spiritually.

The Mormons did not undertake the greatest migration of a people in the history of this nation to seek personal riches and opportunity. Their movement was a result of religious beliefs. In this sense the trek was unique and rightfully compared, as they often took solace in doing, to the exodus of the ancient camp of Israel from bondage in Egypt to the promised land.

The Mormons struggled and suffered through extreme deprivation and hardship because they believed God was with them and their purpose was just. This did not rid their travels, camps and associations of the common distractions and human foibles of other westward emigrants. But, as a whole, the community's response to its condition was remarkable.

The travelers of the original Mormon Trail left an inspiring example for all of us who travel on our own trails through the mortal experience.

# BIBLIOGRAPHY

Black, Susan Easton, and William G. Hartley, eds. *The Iowa Mormon Trail: Legacy of Faith and Courage.* Orem, Utah: Helix Publishing Co., 1997.

*Explore Iowa's Historic Mormon Trails.* Iowa Mormon Trails Association, 1997.

## RELATED PUBLICATIONS

Kimball, Stanley B. *The Mormon Pioneer Trail.* Trail guide published by The Mormon Trail Association, n.d.

Kimball, Stanley B. *Mormon Trail, Voyage of Discovery: The Story Behind the Scenery.* Las Vegas, Nevada: KC Publications, Inc., 1995.

Slaughter, William W. and Michael Landon. *Trail of Hope.* Salt Lake City, Utah: Shadow Mountain, 1997.

# List of Sites in Iowa by County

*(Interpretive panel sites are shown in **bold**)*

## LEE COUNTY

Fort Madison
Old Fort Madison
Keokuk
   Rand Park
Montrose
   **Linger Longer Park**
   **Riverview Park**
Shimek State Forest

## VAN BUREN COUNTY

Bentonsport
   Mason House Inn
**Bonaparte**
Keosauqua
   **County Courthouse**
   Latter-day Saints Visitors and Family History Center
Lacey-Keosauqua State Park

## DAVIS COUNTY

**Bloomfield**
**Drakesville Park**
Lake Wapello State Park
West Grove

## APPANOOSE COUNTY
**Chariton River Crossing**
Iconium
**Lake Rathbun**
Milledgeville

## WAYNE COUNTY
Allerton
Corydon
    **Prairie Trails Museum**
**Tharp Cemetery**
Locust Creek

## LUCAS COUNTY
**Chariton (2)**
Grave Hollow
Red Haw State Park
Stephen's State Forest

## DECATUR COUNTY
Garden Grove
    **Trailside Historical Park (2)**
Lamoni
Nine Eagles State Park

## CLARKE COUNTY
Osceola
    **Clarke County Historical Museum**
**Murray**

## UNION COUNTY
Afton
Creston
Green Valley State Park

**Mt. Pisgah**
**Threemile Lake**

## ADAIR COUNTY

Greenfield
**Mormon Trail Park**
**Orient**

## CASS COUNTY

Atlantic
Cold Springs State Park
Lake Anita State Park
**Lewis (2)**
**Lyman**

## POTTAWATTAMIE COUNTY

Council Bluffs
   **School for the Deaf (2)**
   **Kanesville Tabernacle**
   National Western Historic Center
Lake Manawa State Park
**Macedonia**
Omaha
   Winter Quarters